AROSEINBLOOM

WRITTEN BY JODY BRYANT

AROSEINBLOOM

Copyright © 2024 by Jody Bryant.

All rights reserved. No part of this book may be reproduced in any form or by any electronic or mechanical means, including information storage and retrieval systems, without permission in writing from the publisher, except by reviewers, who may quote brief passages in a review.

This publication contains the opinions and ideas of its author. It is intended to provide helpful and informative material on the subjects addressed in the publication. The author and publisher specifically disclaim all responsibility for any liability, loss, or risk, personal or otherwise, which is incurred as a consequence, directly or indirectly, of the use and application of any of the contents of this book.

MILTON & HUGO L.L.C.
4407 Park Ave., Suite 5
Union City, NJ 07087, USA

Website: www.miltonandhugo.com
Hotline: 1- 888-778-0033
Email: info@miltonandhugo.com

Ordering Information:
Quantity sales. Special discounts are available on quantity purchases by corporations, associations, and others. For details, contact the publisher at the address above.

Library of Congress Control Number:	2024918963
ISBN-13: 979-8-89285-219-7	[Paperback Edition]
979-8-89285-220-3	[Digital Edition]

Rev. date: 09/06/2024

AROSEINBLOOM

WRITTEN BY JODY BRYANT

FOREWORD

Jody and I have known each other since the fall of 2016. It has been an absolute pleasure to be a part of the melting pot that is his creativity and expression. For a lot of our counterparts, being able to create seems so far-fetched and difficult, but not for Jody. Since the day we met, I've witnessed him display his superpower-like creativity in so many forms. Whether it be music or writing, he's always been able to create pieces that grab the consumers' attention and leave their consciousness intoxicated. Every song, album, or poem seems like a unique collectible that was made specifically for you and that's exactly what AROSEINBLOOM is. Each piece within this body of work speaks to the forgotten parts of us that we've neglected to feed overtime. Jody's work does exactly what we've forgotten to continue to do, feed our souls. Piece by piece, you will grow to feel internally and eternally fulfilled. Creators like Jody don't come around often, so having bodies of work such as AROSEINBLOOM available for consumption is beyond a blessing, it's a godsend

-Q.

TABLE OF CONTENTS

MUSE	1
REWIND	3
IS THERE A HEART IN THE HOUSE TONIGHT?	4
'SCUSE ME	5
4 GIVE ME	7
YFM?	8
BROWN SKIN	9
CHILD 'HOOD	11
SUNSHINE	13
eARTh	14
CAN I LOVE YOU?	15
KWESTCHINS	16
BALANCE	17
EVERYTHING WITH GRACE	18
P's & PEONIES	19
WHAT'S LOVE?	20
TALES OF THE LEGEND CALLED "THE GIRL WITH THE TATTOO"	23
COME WALK WITH ME	24
HEAVEN 4 ME	25
3 AM IN DURHAM	26
FORBIDDEN	28
I	29
SOUNDS OF YUE & EYE	30
WHERE I'M FROM	31
ETERNAL	32
THE CRACK IN THE EARTH	33
WE DON'T LOVE THE SAME	34

FALLING… WITH STYLE	35
PERFECTLY IMPERFECT PILLARS	36
U.G.L.Y.	38
EVEN STEVENS	40
FRIEND OR FAUX	42
BUDS & PETALS	44
HEAL	45
DOWNS & UPS	46
LETTER TO MY NEPHEWS	47
THE WALKING WALKMAN	49
LIFE, CAMERAS, ACTIN'	50
THRU MY EYES	51
NAHLIDGE & PEESE	52
BREATHE, ASSESS, REPEAT	53
SMS (SEND ME SOMETHIN')	54
THE FLYING CATERPILLAR	55
AT THE SHORE	57
YOU, THE GREAT	58
IT'S OKAY	59
INSOMNIMANIC	60
BRIGHTER	62
LET YOUR HAIR DOWN	63
WORDS FROM KATHERLEEN	64
BELIEVE	65
4 THE FELLAS	66
AFFIRM	67
UPENDO	68
1801 LOVERS LANE	69
AIRBNB (AN INTROSPECTIVE RECAP ON THE BROWNSTONE 'N BROOKLYN)	70
THE LIL' INSECURE HOMIE	71
BE & SEE	73
INFINITAS VIRES	74
LIFE	75

DEDICATION

I'd like to express my deepest gratitude to so many people so I'm going to do my best to not leave anyone out, but if I do, please charge it to my mind and not my heart. When I decided to embark on this journey of writing my first book, I was high on shrooms on the bottom level of a brownstone in Brooklyn. There I was, 941 miles away from my residence, 839 miles away from home, juggling the overwhelming lessons of love, loss, life and the balance between the three.

I sat in a chair in the corner of the living room with my headphones on while one of my best friends, Q, occupied the television. Eager to experience the high that would soon consume my conscious in a whirlpool of thoughts and emotions, I turn on one of my favorite songs ever composed, Reasons by Earth, Wind and Fire. As the rhythmic sounds of trumpets bellow through, the confines of preconceived notions, doubts and concerns began to crumble as if it were the Berlin Wall. The sounds began to move through my mind like colors. A hi-hat was now a reoccurring pop of ochre. The melody morphed from an arrangement of notes to splashes of bright periwinkle and magenta. The bass line rung through my cerebral cortex, flushing my nervous system with bouts of saffron and hickory. For the first time in my life, I had found words to put to the feelings that rendered me an outcast amongst my peers. And I was too high to tell anyone. As the music continued, I reached over to retrieve the Eric B. & Rakim vinyl that I had just purchased earlier that day to roll another blunt on. Q looked over with sincere concern for my wellbeing as I prepared my ingredients for consumption. "Nigga, stop! You gon' die if you hit that" he exclaimed with a playful laugh which signified that the herbal essence was beginning to settle in with him as well. Little did he know, the person he knew before was already dead.

I stepped outside while the wind whipped across my face, now listening to the songs we had just recorded at Quad Studios a few hours earlier. I paced back and forth, unconsciously plotting. It was like I saw all these puzzle pieces scattered across the floor of my mind. I knew they all fit, it was just up to me to make it all connect. Although I was ecstatic to have accomplished something that was unprecedented in my environment, I still felt unfulfilled. That led to a small moment of frustration within me because how in the world can you still feel empty like you just didn't live the dream? How can you sell short the one experience you've been acting out in your bathroom mirror for the last 15 years? What more could you possibly want? By this point, I'm halfway through my backwood and these thoughts are making me feel mentally claustrophobic. There was no escaping the emptiness, regardless of how high I tried to get. There was no escaping the loneliness, no matter how many songs I recorded. There was no more ignoring this void, a void that needed to be filled with an outlet of a different approach. Just as the answer appeared in my mind, Brooklyn Zoo by Ol' Dirty Bastard of the infamous Wu-Tang Clan crept through my left and right ear creating a head on collision with the idea of writing a book. It all began to make sense. I was lacking a challenge. I was lacking an authentic, unsaturated expression of my raw experiences. The phoenix was rising from the blunt ashes and entering a rebirth phase.

So many beautiful minds played a major role in this realization, beginning with my big sister Nia. My first best friend, bully, therapist, tutor, coach and role model. The one who would always get me into trouble but also did everything in her power to get me out most times. She was the first person in my immediate family (and probably the entire family) to become a published author and so naturally, I looked to her for advice as I embarked on this journey. I thank her for not only loving me unconditionally, but also giving me a foot up my ass when I needed it. Although I didn't always agree with her methods and choices, she instilled certain qualities in me at a very early age that catapulted me into adulthood with a clear head and an open heart. One of the hardest days was when I left to move to Charlotte, and I had to say goodbye to her. I was fighting back tears in front of Q's car when she pulled up. She walked over and wiped my face and gave me a hug that I channel whenever I'm homesick. I told her right then, "if you need me to stay, I will. I'll drop all this shit right now and come home." She smiled as the tears welled up in her eyes and said "nah bro, I couldn't let you do that. You got to start living for you now, we'll be okay. I promise." Thank you for letting me go, I wouldn't have ever found out how high I could fly if you didn't cut me loose.

My baby sister Jasmine, who in fact is not a baby anymore, is without a doubt the second biggest influence for this book. Here we have an individual who taught me how to become a nurturer, a best friend, a bully, a therapist, a tutor, a coach, a role model and all the above when she was just a little girl. Jasmine always kept me on my toes from the day she came home to this very moment as I'm writing this. It is my belief that God gives us people for intended reasons and I'm inclined to believe that God gave me Jasmine so that I will forever be a student. Forever adapting, evolving, learning and growing. Jasmine taught me how to use my words because at a point I had to learn how to connect with her, just like Nia had to learn how she could connect with me. This forced me to really understand that real love can be taxing, but it is always worth it. Jas and I have an 18, going on 19, year-old handshake that we still do without a second thought. Whenever I get a chance to see her, I'm immediately reminded of that little girl that had her own way of doing things. Never following the wave because she felt at ease going against the grain. This little ball of fire inspired me to live unapologetically in my own truth, no matter who agrees or sees the vision. For that, among countless other things, I love you and I thank you from the bottom of my heart for being there for me the day I left for college. "Stay golden, Ponyboy."

These next two individuals are the reason why I am here to begin with. My mother, Monique, and my father, Stanley, are two of the hardest working people you will ever meet in your life. This book took so much out of me, mentally, emotionally, physically, etc. and I know I only got through it mainly because of the work ethic my parents ensured was embedded deep within me. They personify the even balance between life and love for me so in a way, this book is kind of loosely based around them and the lessons I learned from watching them, learning more about them as I got older and rehearing the stories I didn't really care for as a child. Like most children, my parents and I have had several differences growing up. Some, I understand better now that I'm an adult. Others, I forgive them for because they were truly doing the best that they could with limited understanding and resources, a failing economy and three mouths to feed in the heart of inner-city Fayetteville, North Carolina. My father was an artist who shared the same air as tenacious acts like Heavy D and Smokey Robinson. My mother was a lover of the arts as well, having been a writer her whole life and heavily convinced that she would inevitably become Mrs. Michael Jackson. I thank you both for loving me as much as you could, sacrificing the little you had to show us the happiness you wish you could've experienced as children and giving me the genes to be what I have and will become. I love you both with all that I am.

The next person that I must show big love to is my dear friend Zion. I don't have enough space to write out the words that it would take to explain what you mean to me and this entire process but just know that absolutely none of this would be possible without you, Rat, Mr. Darryl, Mrs. Shirley & Mr. Donald. I could name a thousand other people because of you alone but we don't have the time nor space. I met Zion when I was 19 and we've been joined at the hip ever since. There were times where I wasn't always the best person towards you, and I want to use this space to publicly acknowledge that. You've inspired me to become more than I ever imagined I could. From getting kicked out of school, to my first apartment, to getting evicted from said apartment, you were there through it all. After I was suspended and they kicked me out of my dorm, you would lay on my lap and sleep with me on the couch in the common area of your building some nights. That was when I knew one day I would have to tell the world just how amazing you are. I have probably a million more stories about the selfless acts you've done for me but to keep it short I'll leave it at this. Thank you for always being you. You being your authentic self has showed me time and time again that it's easier that way. I love you from this lifetime to the next.

To my Worldwind family, Mudd, Bam, Myles, Nate, Yasir and Q, I thank you all from the bottom of my heart for allowing me to share this journey with you all. I never had brothers growing up but it's safe to say I've adopted y'all as siblings. We even bicker like it from time to time but it's only because we want the absolute best for each other. Q, thank you for letting me get that blanket that night. Who knew our dynamic would blossom into what it has become. Mudd, thank you for being the wisdom that I needed when I was 18 just trying to make it to the next morning. You will never know the influence you had on me, man. Room 311 got me to 9th Wonder and DMC because you gave me a space to grow. Myles, thank you for taking a chance on someone who was just working the grill at McDonald's with you. You will forever be a key component to the magic that was made in the city and soon the world will know just what I mean. Nate, thank you for being a mirror for me. You remind me so much of myself that it's crazy. Never stop pushing the envelope because you have everything you need to be successful already inside of you. Yasir, thank you for being my first little brother. I met Yasir when I was in 10th grade, and he was in 9th and our friendship blossomed into brotherhood almost immediately. You are a wizard with everything you touch so never allow anyone to dim that light. Last but certainly not least, Bam. Thank you. Thank you for the Pontiac. Thank you for the Cookout trays. Thank you for all the pick-ups and drop offs. Thank you for Summer '17. Thank you for not switching up on me when everyone else left me out to dry with the whole TB situation. Thank you for not switching up after the Bainbridge situation when the same people who would sit in my house to smoke would try to play me behind my back. We see how that played out for them. Thank you for being a brother by true definition.

Scrappy. Thank you for believing in that 14-year-old new face that infiltrated your life in the wildest fashion. From mean mugging each other in my auntie's front yard to being my roommate and still one of my best friends 10 years later, I thank you brother. I could get into some wild details about our dynamic as well, but I'll just save that for the next book.

Charli and Korri. Thank you both for being such an inspiration and an asset to my creative process over the last few months. I had absolutely no intentions of going to New York City and making new friends but here we are. Charli, you are a sniper behind the lens, an amazing friend and I can't thank you enough for making sure we didn't get robbed. But seriously, I believe you will be the visionary of what tomorrow will see so never let up and most importantly, never ever let anyone distort your destiny. Thank you for reminding me to breathe. Korri, thank you for coming through how you came through for the kid. Your experiences and wisdom of the world around you provided a perspective that I wasn't accustomed to. Keep inspiring the minds of the future and being a light. Thank you for your ear.

Mrs. Africa, thank you for believing in me before you ever really knew me. I remember when I first met Q, he spoke about you with so much reverence and admiration. If it's one thing about Q, he doesn't play about his mama. When I met you, you hugged me like I was one of your children. In so many ways, you reminded me of the love my mama and grandma used to give me when I was a young boy. I won't lie like I never got your baby boy into some pretty compromising situations, but you can rest assured that I never left him there to fend for himself and I always made sure if no one else did, he would always make it back to you the way he left you. Even if it meant at the expense of my very life. In my formative years, I witnessed first-hand the difficulties that come with being the only boy in a single mother household. I suppose I felt, and still feel, protective of you because the unhealed parts of the child in me sees you how I saw my mama. For what it's worth, Q has you on his back and I got him on mine. Thank you for making Q go to college, thank you for being a strong black woman, thank you for all the sacrifices you made because they remind me that behind every accomplished black man, is a proud black mama.

Mema and Poppi, I love you both and can't thank you enough for giving the girls and I a home and keeping us together. When everything hit the fan in 2010, I was engulfed in uncertainty. You both gave me the love I didn't realize I needed. You were tough when you needed to be and gave me room to breathe easy. I miss you Mema, I'm sorry I wasn't there. Thank you, Poppi, for teaching me discipline, tradition and always making me feel special. Thank you both for reiterating the selflessness that comes from true love.

If I left anyone out, I love you just the same and I appreciate you more than I can mention.

Dedicated to Micah.

Stay dangerous.

MUSE

Muse.
A person or
personified
force who is
the source, of
inspiration. In
tune with the
destination.
Present during
isolation.

Desired when
patience
has expired.
Inquired
by those
who admire
authenticity.
A fantasy
chiselled in
the fallacy of
a harsh reality,
that we are twin flames from 2 different wicks. Chemically compatible just not enough to stick. Days like this make me sick. Knowing you think about me just as often as I daydream about you. Pretending as if the other would *exist less* if we became embedded in the bed that was made prior to our knowledge of the other's *existence*.

Your poker face is commendable to say the least.
I still remember the first time I heard you speak.
The frequency went through both ears and straight to my soul.
Penetrating the insecurities that brandished mechanisms instilled in me from 2006.
You flipped a switch,
soon as your lips greeted me.

Muse.
You barely know me & yet,
you know me all too well.
Visit my dreams again soon.
Consume my energy in the aroma of honeysuckle & cocoa butter.

Your embrace is my place of refuge.
My cocoon will always accept you.
Relinquish the preconceived notion that I'll neglect you.
I want to respect you.
Be numb to everyone except you.
Split the spliff on Neptune & make the universe our rec' room.

Miles Davis "Blue in Green"

REWIND

Hopeless with my romance.
Spontaneous combustion when we hold hands,
to slow jams
that seem like they were made for us.
Love left a stain on us.
And turned into the pain
that started changing us.
Unrequited love inside the Dutch's I be flaming up
when vices kept me company.
And now you fit so comfortably
behind the levees I produced
when darkness tried to come for me.
But still,
I look at you like higher ground
whenever it's flooding inside my mental,
and the slightest sound
can turn into clutter that clogs my pencil.
When you're not around,
you circulate my mind.
Feel a flutter in your spine
soon as we connect,
& then we hit rewind.

John Coltrane "A Love Supreme, Pt. 1: Acknowledgement"

IS THERE A HEART IN THE HOUSE TONIGHT?

Cross all boundaries for me.
Show me sides of you that he would never understand.
Paint my harsh nature with the beautiful hue of your enlightened spirit.
A whirlwind romance but on the exterior? We're "friends. "

I catch myself dreaming daily of you.
Replaying the seconds you spent in my element.
Captivating your energy not only as a man,
But that which is a pillar of regal strength & eloquence.
Melanated excellence.
Eminently defined by my diligence.
So much so, that the Most High & I have a striking resemblance.

You strike me like a match as the type to play the back.
Scoping out the scenery before you get attached.
Partially extroverted.
Obviously photogenic.
A virtuous deity,
Your eyes are so acidic.
But good for me & sweet like orange juice in the morning
While cracking jokes about how your breath stinks when you're yawning.

So as for now, I'm patient.
Understanding of your current situation.
See, I don't pray for devastation in y'all's relation.
I'm just saying.
Home isn't necessarily all about where you be laying.
So, tell me.
Is there a heart in the house tonight?

Weldon Irvine "Morning Sunrise"

'SCUSE ME

I wanna hear about the first time you saw your favourite flower,
because basic icebreakers will never do.
Fuck your favorite color & your favorite tv shows too.
Those aren't the main ingredients,
Let Me Prove My Love to You
by taking an expedition to the sides of you that even you never knew existed.
Let's explore them together.
You're as important as ever.
No question, I'm feeling you.

I wanna hear about the first time you felt you were truly beautiful.
Like the moment you saw yourself outside of your frame.
Outside of the glass case that everyone claims,
doesn't exist when in fact it does
cause you found L'Oréal to mask a grudge,
against the niggas that teased you cause you're black as fuck,
& now it's a *trend* to love *black women*
Except the ones who don't look "black enough."
Like what the *actual* fuck?

I wanna hear about your insecurities.
And not the cute ones.
I mean the ones that make you wanna stay inside and hide from the world around you.
I want you to ask me my opinion on what shoes you should wear.
I promise I won't reply "you know, the cute ones."
I'll say, "the ones that personify your flair and subtracts you from the saturated world around you."

I wanna see you how you see you so I can see how you digest it when I tell you that you're beautiful.
I wanna fall in love the same way you fall in love so when we're done falling, the landing is mutual.
If it isn't painfully obvious yet, I wanna grow old with you.
I wanna be the one to hold you, mold you and console you.
I never wanna be somebody you feel is trying to control you.
I wanna be somebody you trust and lust for just the same.
So, before you walk out of my dreams, what's your name?

Kem "Share My Life"

4 GIVE ME

I pray we meet on the beach, towards the brink of eternity.
On the cusp of forever,
I'll wait for you certainly.
With arms extended wide,
anticipating your embrace.
Internally I collapse
at the glimpse of your face.

A face I once viewed as a beacon
of hope.
That loved me emphatically -
desolate & broke.
The Greeks define this love as
"agape".
Unconditional.

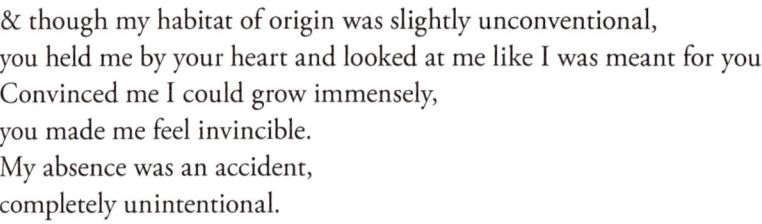

& though my habitat of origin was slightly unconventional,
you held me by your heart and looked at me like I was meant for you.
Convinced me I could grow immensely,
you made me feel invincible.
My absence was an accident,
completely unintentional.

I left you there.
With nothing but empty promises of my return.
But time waits for no one, and this I had to learn.
Unfortunately, at the expense of our permanent disconnect,
so, before you tell me it's okay -
allow me to interject.

I pray we meet on the beach,
on the cusp of forever,
just so I can tell you like I've always wanted,
you made me better.

T.I. *"Still Ain't Forgave Myself"*

YFM?

I want love.
The kind that lets us be ourselves, together.
Engulfed in the bond to which we are tethered,
yet valiant are my efforts towards learning you forever.

I want peace.
I found it from within first but still I was missing something.
The type that you emit effortlessly in abundance,
that I'll still find inside your eyes when we're well into our hundreds.

I want you.
Yes, you soothe my flesh but we're symmetrical in energy.
Though our connection is familiar like a fading core memory,
I pray in the next lifetime your soul will still remember me.

You feel me?

A.$.A.P Ferg (feat. Brent Faiyaz) "Dreams, Fairytales, Fantasies"

BROWN SKIN

Brown Skin.

Fixated on the contours of your full lips as they danced in slow motion to the rhythm of the pronunciation of your name. Deafened by the blare of infatuation, I smiled to elude the fact that my ears heard nothing. Yet, my body heard everything. Responding by making my heart race at such an intense pace, I get winded just from the sight of your face.

Brown Skin.

I call you that not to objectify you but mainly because I'm far too embarrassed to ask for your name again.
See, rather than gathering the same quotes & applying the same approach as a common man would.
I'd rather address you as something more.
An ochre-bathed jewel manufactured by the prophecy of our ancestors.
Sun-kissed in the blend of hazelnut and honey.
Chiseled and chipped to the likeness of Aphrodite,
Dipped in the essence of Venus.
An effervescent Negus such as I would turn shy in the presence of a goddess so fly.

Brown Skin.

Can I have just another moment of your time before you run off to reality again?
Leaving me to replay every detail about you.
From the way your eyes pierce through the frame of my mind to your hair being a direct reflection of how you're feeling that day.
I'd be lying if I said I didn't want you in every kind of way.
I just wish you could stay, Brown Skin.

Anita Baker "Sweet Love"

CHILD 'HOOD

Antenna on top of the tv
Pliers for knob
1987 Grand National with the system that makes you bob

Whenever they come through
We would watch 'em from off the stoop
& give our bikes a model type
Thought my lil' bitch was a
Coupé

The way I scoot
Away from yappin' Ma Dukes
I was on the move
Scrappin'
Throwing my dukes
& every time I lose
I doubled back for round 2
& I ain't going home
My losses taught me how to see it through

When my father sees my bruises
I'll be up till 'round 2
Throwing punches till my arms cramp
It's really nothing new

Adolescent down a bumpy road
This shit was nothing smooth
When they fell from off that pedestal
I sunk into a groove
& found truth

I document the days of my youth
Inside a composition
Composed on instrumental loops
Granny's rice pudding was the proof
The world was my zoo
A lot of sisters kept it real, but not as real as my 2

Plus 4
Blade to jugular
The world is cutthroat
People tell you go to college
& never tell you what for
I learned more politicking with the homies through blunt tokes
& walking outside
Consumed in the smell of the gun smoke.

Scarface "On My Block"

SUNSHINE

You don't just shine bright,
Your glow illuminates me,
You make sure I'm seen.

Nipsey Hussle "4 in the Mornin"

EARTH

From dirt we are made,
Washed and renewed by the water,
To dirt we return.

Marvin Gaye "If I Should Die Tonight"

CAN I LOVE YOU?

I loved you until I hated myself.
I loved you when there was nobody else.
I loved you because you were you.
I loved you, through and through.

I loved you when you fucked the nigga I "DiDn'T hAvE tO wOrRy AbOuT."
I loved you before I had a hammock and a furnished house.
I loved you when the homies told me to leave you alone.
I loved you still, even after you left me on my own.

I loved you so much, I chose every word carefully.
I loved you so much, I never moved carelessly.
I loved you so much, I smiled to keep the peace.
I loved you so much, I forgot that I was me.

I loved you when I had every reason not to.
I loved you even after I got you.
I loved you, all of you, despite your past.
I loved you even when I had to ask,

Can I love you?

Gladys Knight & The Pips "Neither One of Us"

KWESTCHINS

Why you always gotta think?
Have you ever felt love?
Why you never hit the club?
Why you feel like you gon' sink?

Why you always gotta shrink?
Have you ever rose above?
Why you never need a hug?
Why you stutter when you blink?

Why you always gotta lie?
Have you ever kept it real?
Why you never yourself?

Jadakiss (feat. Anthony Hamilton) "Why"

Be still,

Allow time to do its' thing.

Leave distractions and fears behind,

Although the disconnect will sting.

Never cower or run from problems,

Capture memories with every glance, &

Even if you end with nothing, at least you took the time to dance.

Lee Ann Womack
"I Hope You Dance"

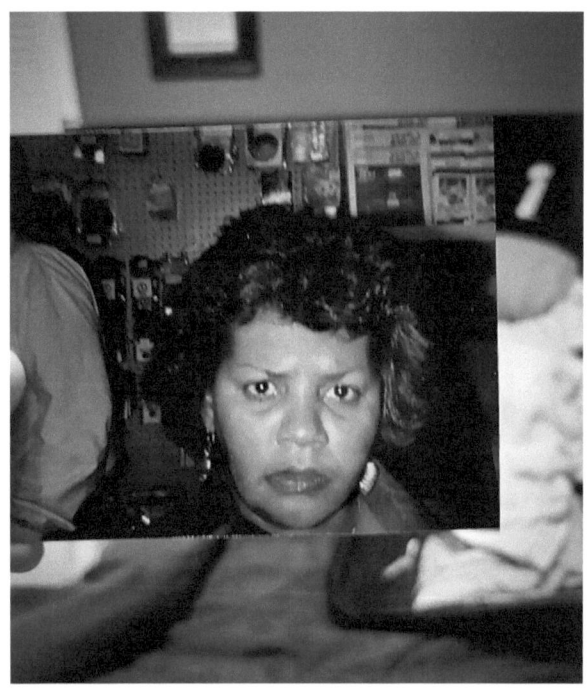

EVERYTHING WITH GRACE

Remember to give yourself grace.
You aren't as bad as you think.
What good is being first in a race,
When it's over as soon as you blink?

Remember to take it easy,
Be still and count to 10,
And if you're still uneasy,
Just count to 10 again.

Remember to just be you.
Think before you speak.
When overthinking makes you blue,
Crying doesn't make you weak.

UMI "Breathe"

P's & PEONIES

I looked into the sun.
She blinded me at first with her vivacious rays that penetrated my Teflon exterior.
Caused me to perspire every ounce of moisture within me as we got closer.
Eternally locked in her
gravitational pull, we even each other out like covalent bonds.
The attractive and repulsive.
The proactive and reactive.
The sweet and the bitter.
All working hand and hand against the societal standard that opposites
could never waltz deliriously to the melodies of their differences.

I looked into the sun.
Her warmth made me miss her more when all the moon had to offer was a wave and a little light.
The moon only gives me all of her here and there, most times I only get half.
But the sun?
She shows her vibrancy every day,
and only gets dimmed when the moon is in the way.

Beenie Man "Girls Dem Sugar"

WHAT'S LOVE?

Love is how you give
Barely what it is
Love is what you take
When destiny and fate correlate
And align
Love is spending time
See, you can spend a dime, but the effort is what simmers in her mind
Bottom line
Love is tough convos and honesty
Love letters written anonymously
Explaining that I don't know where I would be at
Without ya
Love is being thankful for the time I spend around ya
Love is what we got
Even if somebody takes my spot

Love is not even explaining how we rock
And even when I rot
And they put peonies over my plot
I pray that love fills the places where I'm not
Love is like the Glock
That left Ace Boogie leaking from his top
Love is pain that'll leave you stuck in shock
Love is what Keisha had for Tommy when the feds came
Love is when y'all fuckin and fuck up another bed frame
Crazy with head games
Love can really do that
Love is getting high with the homies freestyling over "Who Dat"
Love is getting therapy
Big love to the ones carried me
When I ain't love myself
Love is getting help when you need it

And when you feel defeated
Know I got the kinda love that won't
Leave you depleted
I mean it and I mean it for real
Love can make you chill
And I love you cause you loving me still
For real

Love is from the soul
Connected by the stories untold
We progress as we let love unfold
The corners of our mind
Love can take you anywhere with time
You know I love it when I see my people shine
Love is how we talk
But more importantly, it's how we walk
God forbid, I get outlined with chalk
Love is in my spirit
As far as death
It's no reason to fear it
Move with love so my conscience is the purest
Love can make you change
And reassess the way you play the game
Love is balance between joy & the pain
Love is more than passion
Love is only real when it's in action
If you love me, give me wisdom where I'm lacking
Love tastes like honey
And feels like butterflies in your tummy
Love is real when it ain't based off my money
I love the way you think
I love the way you rock a hoodie like a mink
I love you so much that I hate I have to blink
Cause I don't want to miss a thing
Love can leave your mind captivated
Love is when your "weird side" is activated
Love will never be outdated
Love is when your partner feels the safest

In your presence
Because the essence of your presence is a blessing
And they hate it
Whenever you must leave out in a rush
Love is when your smile makes them want to blush
Love is such a skill
I mean it and I mean it for real
I just love you cause you're loving me still
For real

Erykah Badu "Other Side of the Game"

TALES OF THE LEGEND CALLED "THE GIRL WITH THE TATTOO"

Drawn to you like it was illustrated by Basquiat or Picasso
Your skin latches to mine like Velcro
My eyes run bashfully from yours to the floors surrounding our feet
You grab my chin gently to readjust my attention
"Focus on me"
I never dreamed of the day
That I would be comfortable enough to say
I've never been adored this way
& I'm too frightened to fully commit to the feeling
Instead, I'm accustomed to feeling like I'm not worth something so appealing
And now we lay here as I'm staring at the ceiling
Daydreaming about the days I daydreamed of you
Silently thanking God for paying attention when I prayed to spend time with someone like you
With eyes closed, our heartbeats compose harmonies in colors like fluorescent pink and jazz blue
The love we make will awake the heavens and sacredly be known as tales of the legend called "The Girl with the Tattoo"

Miguel "The Girl With the Tattoo Enter.lewd"

COME WALK WITH ME

I was awakened from my sleep by the sounds of the street
I could barely hear the birds like I used to
Took a shower, brushed my teeth
The same morning routine
Switchblade for them hot heads that cruise through
On my dresser by my brush
Tie my shoes in a rush
And I'm gone with the wind like its Broadway
As I'm heading out the door, I say a prayer to the lord that I make it back
Cause niggas shoot in broad day
6:30 in the morning
I don't want to ride the bus cause they got us sitting 3 to a seat
So in lieu of being stuck
I'm out before the sun is up
Trying to make it to my school on feet
Most of my peers had whips
And parents that gave them shit
Living life without a care in the world
I'm not saying that with hate
One day, I'm gon' be a great
So my son ain't getting rides from his girl
But for now, I'm still grinding
You know pressure makes a diamond
And the gems I possess gon' shine
Soon they'll all gravitate
First, I gotta graduate
So, for now I'm just taking my time

Kanye West "Last Call"

HEAVEN 4 ME

If heaven had a slum
Where a young nigga could run
Like when he did back when he was just a child
Resilience in his smile
And the sun would never set to the sound
of a tech blast
Collect cash is operation 1
Operation 2 is get my boo & have a daughter or a son
And train 'em while they're young
How to avoid the shit that I have done
And be the one to show 'em how to overcome
The projects felt like home
The scenery for memories I've known
So, I imagine when my physical is gone
Ima wake up to a street paved with gold
& walk past Impala's that's rolling on 24s
With my halo to the side
And healing from all the tears that I have cried
Run inside of me like IVs
The phoenix is arising
And when it's said and done
And I leave with the breeze
I wanna wake up in the hood next to Adam & Eve
Now let it breathe

DMX "Slippin'"

3 AM IN DURHAM

Me and CJ was outside when the block had a curfew
Before he had the tinted Ford Escape trynna swerve through
Hwy 7 7 hitting Cookout to kill time
Knowing any moment that somebody could steal mine
But that's the risk you run
When you're young
With ambition
Two months before I turned my tassel
Letter from admissions
Came inside the mail
I excelled at the buzzer
Now all I gotta do is try and make it through the summer
And I'll be off to college with my own bed
Mani could come and visit
Just to kick it
While my phone dead
But
Instead of having to wait for me
She had vacancies
And wasn't trynna be tied down
And so, we broke it off
Now I'm broken hearted
CJ tried to solve it
Money is the root of all evil
But now it's like the solvent
Dissolving all my problems
Through penitentiary chances
We numb to our conditions
We're in anemones dancing
Like
Latrell at the Hamptons
We pulled up to a light
Where we usually make a right
But he kept it going straight & said "I'm finna get you right"
I trust him with my life

For the moments I'll never write
So, I hit the blunt
And listened to the isms and advice
He was laying down over ice
Like the cool nigga he is

After while I noticed that we pulled up to a crib
A side of town I never been
Now my nerves jumping outta my skin
But still, I hold it in
My vision blurry as fuck cause I'm fried
Then
CJ stopped talking
Look over his eyes wide
Now
He got a nigga shook off the look
My mouth tried
To get the words out
Then noticed the look
His eyes tied
To the beam that was glued to my chest
Thought I was next
In the lineage of niggas that left
On grass stretched
At the hand of the niggas that flex and blast techs
Pray it jam like my daddy's collection of cassettes

Kendrick Lamar *"Sing About Me, I'm Dying of Thirst"*

FORBIDDEN

I wanna be wrapped in you
The chemistry we manufacture through "lmfao's" & heart reactions
Makes my heart react in
Ways I forgot it could

Finding myself drifting away in the thought of you more often than I'd like to admit
Your exterior
The definition of duality as it transitions from almond milk and honey to sandpaper grit
A defense mechanism indeed but you don't let it intercede whenever it comes to you dealing with me
And I like that

Because you know you're safe here
All sides of you
I wanna know them in depth
I wanna read to you while I rest my head on your chest
And almost pass out from trynna match the pace of your breath
And break your defenses like Steph
When he fakes to the left

But I fall back
Cause you belong to somebody else
That got you put up
Like you belong on somebody's shelf
Never mind the fact I cross your mind and your body melts
I leave you timid
Forbidden, but I still want you to myself

Tyler, The Creator "WILSHIRE"

I

I thrive in isolation
Succeed in solitude
I've spent more nights alone than I spent eating my mamas' food
My pop was on the move
My peers were on the news
And I was stuck between breaking down & trynna break through
Satchmo in the backwood
Satchmo in the background
My nigga dancing with the stars, he's never coming back down
Make it through the pat down
And blow another pack down
My thoughts be hella abstract
Picasso over trap sounds
And lately I've been dealing the thought of being trapped
Cause niggas leave home and very rarely make it back
But ima be the one to put the city on the map
No matter where my feet land I rep the family where I'm at

Juelz Santana "One Day I Smile"

SOUNDS OF YUE & EYE

would you rather be loved for your exterior assets or adored for what treasures lie beneath the surface?
would you call our connection coincidence or claim it as divine purpose?
have you ever been loved without conditions or suffering attached?
what if I Promise on my life the Jagged Edge to our hearts could match?
okay, the last one was corny, but you get the gist right?
I want you under me like the wind & a swift lil' kite.
Instead, I'm feeling like I'm Arthur with his fist clenched tight
cause what I want rings inside my mind daily like bells
so not the fool, I play it cool cause you belong to somebody else.

Prince "Reflection"

WHERE I'M FROM

I'm from where niggas crack under pressure flossing them diamonds.
I'm from where niggas are still waiting on J. Cole to sign 'em.
I'm from where you can get everything from the tobacco store.
I'm from where some be scared to hit niggas but quick to smack a hoe.
I made it out from where I'm from and I ain't going back,
Until I make a name and show I got my dough intact.
A thousand miles from where I'm from is still a little too close.
The heartbreak that I suffered there fucks with me the most.
From death, dishonor, and the detriment of both combined.
I saw the love grow sour and devour precious minds.
I got a homie that's always preaching "knowledge of self,"
Cause where we're from the ignorance will get your presence felt.
Being smart is just the art of how to blend and be aware,
Being dumb is being too smart with niggas who don't care.
Where I'm from, intelligence is measured by your relevance
And the ability to keep it cool when they check your temperament.

Jay-Z "Where I'm From"

ETERNAL

This liquor has the best of me
You've always been a friend to me
A remedy
I love you more than anything
From now until the end of me
Your enemies are my enemies
Connected by our energies
From now until infinity
We fall into forever holding hands
Perfect symmetry

Roddy Ricch "slow it down"

THE CRACK IN THE EARTH

As your heartbeat declined,
There was a moment in time,
Where I heard a crack in the Earth

The days you were mine,
Will live in my mind,
Especially when I forget my worth

Now I lose sleep,
As you rest in peace,
And I'm left to juggle the hurt

Cause you were my world,
Your pain was heard,
I still hear that crack in the Earth.

Big K.R.I.T. *"I Gotta Stay"*

WE DON'T LOVE THE SAME

We don't have the same type of love.
You love me like a dog loves his owner when it's food in the bowl,
I love you like my dawg loved his mama when it wasn't beautiful at home
You're beautiful & grown
Your medulla what I'm on
The way a nigga runnin' through your mind
Like I'm trynna get ahead of the chills that be runnin down your spine
But it's fine
Cause you was never mine
Never mind
In another lifetime
You would probably never mind
The thought of a lifetime
With Jon
I guess we'll never know
Cause right now you see me as a bro
And I'm forced to act like I'm in love with the dough
When the dollars don't make sense if I ain't spending time with you
Independent woman but you're extra good when I'm with you
& I ain't got it all
I can't put you in a cabin for the fall
Or get you everything you want inside the mall
But when monumental moments
Make you feel small
I'm the one you call
Cause I got enough heart
To build impenetrable walls
Around you
You can feel my love all around you
And I gotta watch you give it to the next man
Cause we're just friends

Erykah Badu "Next Lifetime"

FALLING... WITH STYLE

God, we need to talk
And I think it's kinda urgent
Cause I really don't know what I did to deserve this
I wallowed through the urchins & serpents
Trynna find my purpose
And found somebody perfect
I've never been this certain
She laughs at all my jokes
Till she squeezes her sides
I think it's all cap and she be feeding me lies
But then
I look in her eyes
And I see no disguise
And I die a little inside when I be seeing her cry
Oh fuck
I'm falling in love

Lauryn Hill (feat. D'Angelo) "Nothing Even Matters"

PERFECTLY IMPERFECT PILLARS

My father was a theorist
My angle was the purest
I saw that nigga unfold visions inside of mirrors
Rent money on the dresser
He was my first professor
He taught me how to make the most when all we had was lesser
Than everybody else
Back when the trailer park was poppin'
He taught me that having respect could solve most of your problems
The other part is having heart to get you through the dark
You gotta play it smart or get picked apart by the sharks
When they smell you bleeding
Cause boy you gon get cut
But look at all my scars and learn to duck
You know that bob and weave
Like Edna mode
To get the dough
You got the game
Just play it slow
And one day let the world know
I'm Stanley's son
The second coming of a don
The middle boy
The only one
The world is yours
Now gimme some
I throw that nigga dap
& then I hit the road with Scrap
The rest is history
When you listen, I hope you play this back

My mother was a goddess
Fuck trynna keep it modest
I know we had our differences but let's put that aside and
Just focus on the love
I felt through every hug
I used to hear you praying
Still remember you saying
That I had nothing to fear when I hear them bullets sailing
Across my window screen
And then somebody scream
You would grab us and talk to us till we fell asleep
And get us up in the morning like it was all a dream
You always kept us fed
Before we went to bed
No matter if you were hungry
You got up every day to go out there and make the bread
Regardless of what was ahead
It felt like home when you were there
Courageous even if you scared
Cause you're
Nikki's bambino
Warrior of God flow
My mama coproduced with the realest nigga alive bro
When I was born, she held me to the heavens by herself
And said behold
The only thing greater than yourself

John Legend "Ordinary People"

U.G.L.Y.

A consensus of what it is to be
Unpleasant or repulsive
Especially in appearance
Who knew beauty was as hideous as me?
Reflected in my stride
A combination of qualities
However
None aesthetically pleasing to the eye
And even when you try
To fit the mold
That wasn't bestowed
Fake shit will never coincide
With who you are inside
Rather be lame than be a lie
You know that money ain't a thing when you die
and neither is your pride
But be that as it may
I still be high
So I can laugh at all the shit that makes me cry
Alone in my bed with all the lights cut out
Mama talking about a blessing
While we're stressing cause the lights been out
For like 3 weeks
Cutting grass
Bringing in cash
And every day I sit while everybody laughs
At the clothes
That I chose
When they don't even know the half
Could've spazzed
My mama used to whoop my ass
so bad
I had cuts and bruises from my neck to my calves
And still come into class with a grin
Even though the fabric is sticking to the welts on my skin
So it's impossible to learn the best way to make a friend
When you're 12 trynna process the ugly within

But pardon me
I drift on tangents I apologize
The thought of ugly is deceptive
With all kinda lies
I mean really having you thinking shit is one way
When it ain't
Courage says you can do it
Ugly says you can't
Ugly trapping off a mid-pack
Cappin' like it's dank
Knowledge hydrates the soul
Ugly tells you not to drink
Thoughts of being the ugliest duckling
Used to fuck with me
My demons throwin' jabs
But me?
I'm with the fuckery
No longer incarcerated by victim mentality
No longer shrinking myself so niggas ain't mad at me
Utilizing tools from past pain
Working on myself
I love you ugly
You taught me this:
U Gotta Luv Yaself

Anthony Hamilton "Ain't Nobody Worryin'"

EVEN STEVENS

A bitter person
Is a good person
That just never got they're lick back
It's kinda hard to digest
When you never had to sit back
And sip that
And everybody telling you to heal
Feeling crazy when you tell 'em how you feel
Cause they never really seem to get it
When they probably do and don't wanna look crazy too
So, you watch how this feeling takes two
And only one gets relief
Nah nigga not you
Quite the opposite in fact
The cat you impact
Takes facts
 You unpack
And doesn't vent back
Now you stuck on some stupid shit
Your ventilation lucrative
For everybody else
But yaself

Benny the Butcher "Langfield"

My sisters
My mama
Grandmama
My auntie
My bros
The homies
& even people I don't know
All telling me to talk about it
But what's the point of really talking about it
If ain't no bodies being caught about it

That means
Killing the old shit
The hoe shit
The faux shit
The petty lies I unfolded
I'm too real for that
You took my kindness for weakness
And I kinda feel like you're weak for that

FRIEND OR FAUX

I'm the worst kinda friend

            Always clap from afar

                        But don't call & check in

        I don't know what to call it

I've been feeling something crazy

        I've been trynna keep it solid

                So, I kinda cut you off while I solve it

        Hennessy transactions I deposit

To cope with all the losses

        Remember back in college

                Apologies for times I wasn't honest

      Made it seem like I was polishing a diamond

But really, I was searching for myself

        My foundations' a landslide

                My parents cut ties at 9

    So, every connection after that was just a clip on

Fuck you good then get gone

      And fucking you ain't even always about the physical

                    Toxic in my ways because I'm miserable

        Hoping you would never

Uncover

                The fact that

                        I don't really know shit about shit

Phyllis Hyman "Old Friend"

BUDS & PETALS

Roses are
gorgeous
Daisies
are too
My
dedication
to the future
me keeps the
present me
from you

Peonies are
priceless
Tulips as
well
Your
admiration
will dwindle
if I remain
in this shell

Lilies or
orchids?
I cannot decide
Stagnation will hinder my blessing supply

Lotuses are lovely
Camellias are rare
My buds are still blooming, so handle with care

Brent Faiyaz "Been Away"

Heal the places that hurt the most

Embrace the journey with those that are close

Allow yourself a space for grace

Learn to love your style and taste

(REPEAT AS OFTEN AS NEEDED)

Dizzy Gillespie "All the Things You Are"

DOWNS & UPS

Life is filled with various motions.
Mainly, the ups & downs.
Things are beautiful, working smoothly & then they change abruptly.
Altering everything & creating a space of uncertainty.
In these times, rely on the fact that the universe we abide in operates with balance.
For every "down" is an equal & opposite "up".
Therefore, we should change our approach to this inevitable cycle.
Rather than anticipating the "ups" and neglecting the "downs",
Anticipate the proven fact that you will see your "downs" to reach your "ups."
Fall in love with this truth & flourish.

SZA "20 Something"

LETTER TO MY NEPHEWS

Surround your soul with people who help you see how big the world is.
Engage your energy with people who show you how broad your horizon can be.
Engulf your exterior with people who still call you by your government name.

Tame your time by submerging yourself in positivity.
Hear your heart, it speaks quietly so listen tentatively.
Elevate your entity by understanding the significance of self-care.

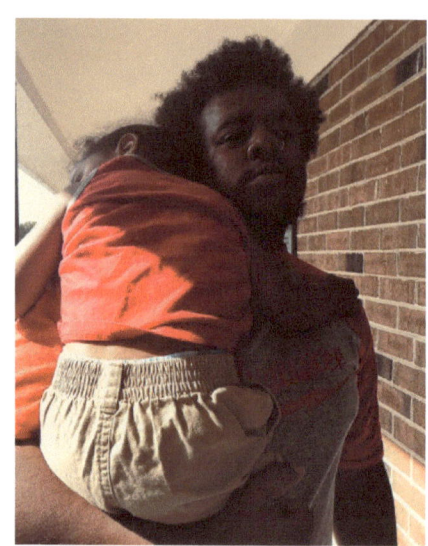

Witness the world through an ever-evolving lens, it's more fun that way.
Own every option you have with intent and confidence.
Read the room, it'll never lie.

Live *YOUR* life to the absolute fullest. You'll sleep better that way, trust me. Divide the dough and invest wisely.

Demand your due respect through your actions. The loudest is the weakest.
Ignore the idiots that will belittle you. People fear what they don't understand.

Find your focus and lock into it. An idle mind doesn't make any money.
Forge a fortress of solitude that you can always access in your mind when home is too far.
Entertain your ego until it becomes detrimental to your growth. Be wise in your confidence.
Remain a responsible and respectful man, even when it doesn't feel pleasant.
Equalize your emotions by working through them. They can be a liability if you don't.
Never ever need someone for something you can do for yourself.
Teach the tots beneath you these lessons and add your own as you grow.
Learn that lies only lead to having to tell more lies to cover the old lies.
You are your own man. I love you, I'm proud of you and always see the world differently.

Jay-Z "Anything"

THE WALKING WALKMAN

Walking is my new thing.
Overwhelmed? Walk.
Overthinking? Walk.
The answers to the uncertainty that looms are found in the steps we never take.
So, start walking & never stop.

Fleetwood Mac
"Dreams"

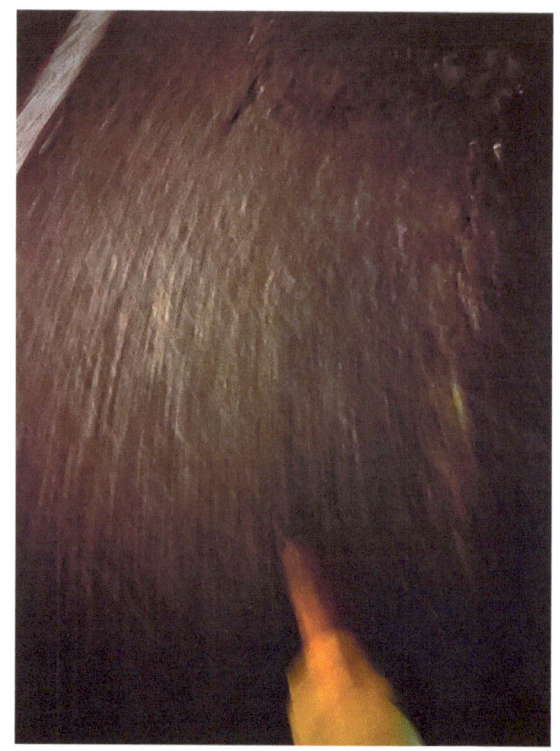

LIFE, CAMERAS, ACTIN'

Life made us great actors.
Constantly portraying the roles of individuals who aren't who we really are.
So much so, that even we tend to forget that this role is just a façade created in comfortability.
Forgetting that we are not this part that we pieced together to maintain normalcy.
And yet, we spend our lives watching people do it for entertainment.
Not even realizing we live tragedies every day that no one will even see.
We just act as if they don't exist.

Amy Winehouse "You Know I'm No Good"

THRU MY EYES

The scent of your favorite perfume wakes me.
The sweet sound of you humming our favorite melody gently enters my conscious.
I am beguiled by your presence alone.
My eyes open and to my surprise, there you are.
Just as you were the day before.
Choosing to infiltrate the parameters of mind,
Painting the corners and spaces that have long been overlooked with a hue that only you can produce.
Sharing my vigilance in the pursuit to mend the ventricles that feed into a heart under rehabilitation.
Being my ventilation.
Taking consideration.
A thriving illustration of God's greatest creation.
You see me watching you in the wall sized mirror that would shatter if it could capture the radiance of your natural aura.
You smile at me with pure jubilation, excited to begin another page in the manuscript we curate day in and day out.
You walk over and connect with my embrace before I even brush my teeth and when I try to duck away you act like my funk brings you peace.
We lay there.
Taking in the moments that will soon become memories.
I am whole within myself.
I am fulfilled with you.
As we continue to lay in harmony with each other's heartbeats.
Speaking fluently through body language.
We dwell outside of the realm of reality and reside so deep within each other's eyes.

Smino (feat. reggie) "Lee & Lovie"

NAHLIDGE & PEESE

Love isn't confounded to the walls of time
Nor is time bound to the whims of man
Both are precious gifts given from God
Value them while you have them at hand

And when your mind is overwhelmed
And troubles infiltrate your peace
Worry not, remain steadfast
Courageous hearts embrace defeat

If ever you're lost, confused or dismayed
In search of purpose to guide your dreams
Trust in the voice that whispers inside you
And capture your destiny by any means

When doubt is near, and hope depletes
And love appears to be outdated
Remember these words I leave with you
Knowledge is power, your peace is worth saving

Duke Ellington & John Coltrane "In A Sentimental Mood"

BREATHE, ASSESS, REPEAT

Thoughts pounding
Anxiety surrounding
Production is what matters most

Heart racing
Feet pacing
Depression is surely close

Vision blurred
Blowing herbs
And then a wise man said to me

"Life is fragile,
Don't be frazzled,
Breathe, assess and then repeat."

Common "Real People"

SMS (SEND ME SOMETHIN')

Something about a woman who loves herself makes me love her more.
Eagerly capturing moments in her world to share with me.
Notably, something about a woman sending an unsolicited selfie makes the sunshine a little brighter.
Defenseless and vulnerable, I'd unapologetically gaze at the attachment for hours and when the homies ask, I'll just act like I'm not attached.

My Heart never misses a beat with the Polaroids.
Enveloping my essence with a segment of instant film.

Seeing your photograph feels as if I can feel you.
Opening my imagination to the numerous ways I could fold you and hold you.
Melanin sparkles through the invisible ink.
Envious of the straps and laces that hug your supple skin.
Thinking of you begins to bring this aroma of vanilla bean & brown sugar to my senses.
Humbled by the fact that you would even bless my phone with such delicacies.
I swear, it's something I love about a woman who loves herself.
Nevertheless, when words fall short, you're right there with the perfect attachment like an
apostrophe.

J. Cole "Photograph"

THE FLYING CATERPILLAR

There once was a caterpillar who believed he could fly
Every day he would climb where the trees met the sky
Above all the birds and bunnies and bees
To a safe little space above all the leaves

Here he would sit with his little eyes shut
And dream about all this magical stuff
Like "when I grow wings I'll fly to the moon,
And you won't hear from me 'til the middle of June!"

The sun would then set, and he'd climb down the tree
To his home to share stories about what he had seen
Excited to tell all these wonderful tales
Of the sights, the sounds and the sweet oaky smells

But to his surprise, nobody believed
One day he would fly like the birds and the bees
Honest-to-goodness, I can't tell a lie
This poor little caterpillar wanted to cry

He inched away sadly as slow as a tortoise
To his favorite tree in the back of the forest
Depressed and ashamed, he barely could speak
Embarrassed by all that he wanted to be

He spun a cocoon for somewhere to hide
And when he was done, he cried inside
Sobbing and wailing, he began to weep
And soon his frustration had put him to sleep

By now, it's been days since our little friend left
And as he awakens, he lets out a stretch
From out the cocoon what had blossomed inside
Was a colorful, beautiful, bright butterfly

He flew by his home for the doubters to see
He soared pass the birds, the bunnies and bees
To live out his days at peace in the sky
As a caterpillar who once believed he could fly

Kanye West "We Don't Care"

AT THE SHORE

The waves of life crash
Against my brittle frame
I am made new again

Frank Ocean "Swim Good"

YOU, THE GREAT

Great things take time to create.
Remember this when you get bent out of shape.
The highs,
The lows,
They come,
And go,
But **you** will
always be great.

*Larry June
"Feeling Good
Today"*

IT'S OKAY

Just let it all go
That's the poem right there
Let the wind take it

Keyshia Cole (feat. Missy Elliot & Lil 'Kim) "Let It Go"

INSOMNIMANIC

Some nights I lay awake & watch the ceiling fan spin
Replaying all the moments in my life that make me cringe
The times that I would lie hoping just to fit in
Played like I was shy then wondered why we're just friends

                        Made myself small trying not to take space
                        Deflecting the attention cause I'm trynna save face
                        The times I stayed quiet cause I needed your embrace
                        And every time I held back cause of what my friends would say

Now here I am, lying beside a beautiful queen
Who's dream nigga is tall like Shaq and Kareem
Who got cream and one day he'll probably give her a ring
Fuck her proper to Big Poppa probably making her cream

                        And I lay awake to plot the blueprint to my escape
                        Out this mediocre mindset that's kept me out of shape
                        Then a thought crept that turned my mental to a vortex
                        A chemical imbalance stuck in my cerebral cortex

Every time I failed infiltrates my cognitive flow
Torment my mental with convictions that I already know
My mind is racing like that Jamaican that won the hundred meter
And I miss my grandmama right now I need her

        Get up out the bed, roll up a blunt while Shawty's sleeping
        Kiss her on the cheek then head outside to feel the breeze and
        Try and clear my mind, I don't know why it works the hardest at night
        They say what's done in the darkness will transcend to the light

So, I expect my work ethic to be impressive when I rise
Check the time
An **_hour_** 'til it's 7:45?
Now I'm fucked
And I don't really wanna test my luck
Exhale deep after I take my last puff

        I shuffled up the steps to close my eyes, practicing lies
        To tell Shawty so she won't see past my brolic disguise
        I cuddle with her as she rests her head back on my arm
        And just as soon as the thoughts stop, I hear my alarm

Lute "Be Okay"

BRIGHTER

When the path is unclear
And hope is diminished
Remain tranquil in knowing
Your story isn't finished

Your skies may darken
And good deeds unnoticed
When these moments arise
Remember and always know this

You aren't your mistakes
Your past doesn't define you
For every setback you encounter
Is a chance to redesign you

Take baby steps
Trust that life will make you wiser
And when dark nights occur
Remember, tomorrow is always brighter

Twista & Faith Evans "Hope"

LET YOUR HAIR DOWN

Things will occur whether we're acclimated or scared
For tomorrow is only the concern of the foolish and unprepared

Concern yourself with only that which you can control
For only within the moment resides our purest soul

On this quest to conquer the obstacles and impediments that lie ahead
Listen twice as much to what is shown and half to what is said

When the noise is overwhelming, and peace is nowhere around
Take your time, relax your mind and just let your hair down

***Corinne Bailey Rae "Put Your Records On"**

WORDS FROM KATHERLEEN

The sun will shine again
The rain will water your harvest

When greatness is at hand
The tests will be the hardest

You can overcome
Your destiny is compelling

Remember that you're the one
And you're constantly excelling

Diana Ross "I'm Coming Out"

Be all you can with all you have

Envision that nothing can stop you

Live as one who perseveres with

Intent, purpose and value

Even then, the trials will come and

Very few will know

Everything you had to do to live your truth and grow

Big Sean "Nothing Is Stopping You"

4 THE FELLAS

Can we all agree that crying is the most uncomfortable, comforting thing… like ever?

Really, it's the hardest, most simple task to accomplish most times.

Yes, I'm talking to you. Let it out, bro.

Lyfe Jennings "Cry"

AFFIRM

I am right where I need to be

I trust myself

I love the person I'm becoming on this journey

I will not allow myself to deter from this path to appease others

I am worthy of love

I will hold myself accountable

I will take another step in my purpose today

I can let go of what doesn't serve my best self

I am not always right

I shine regardless of the adversity I face

Miles Davis "All Blues"

UPENDO

Mother of the earth
The closest thing to God
I love you for being you
And everything you are

Creator of all life
Goddess of the land
You are worthy of admiration
I give you all that I can

Ruler of serenity
Whose wrath is insurmountable
Your love is equally intense
Unconditionally unfathomable

Thank you for your patience
Your kindness and your light
Your love provides the balance
That brings guidance to my life

Musiq Soulchild "Love"

1801 LOVERS LANE

Intimacy in the highest form caresses my mental
Some require more but my weakness is simple
Driven by the happiness I'm trynna get into
Helps me navigate through surface level features that tend to
Distract my vision
Constantly in touch with bad decisions
Search for what I'm missin'
In the same places you caught me slippin'
Trynna find my rhythm
Catching your cadences when you send em'
But mixed signals always throw monkey wrenches inside the middle
Of our common goals
Feelings exposed
Then I go cold
Cause we're just friends
But I see your body outside of clothes
When I'm all alone
And I'll never tell you how much I love you
Cause you got hoes
I used to have bros
I got foes
So, I cling to you
But more like a friend
Less like a lover
Cause I'm needing you
The world is fugazi
And we discover
That nobody else
Can do the things we do for one another
So, tell me why we're acting
As if we aren't terrified without each other

Lauryn Hill "Can't Take My Eyes Off of You"

AIRBNB (AN INTROSPECTIVE RECAP ON THE BROWNSTONE 'N BROOKLYN)

I've spent so much time running.
Hiding from the truths that
sail courageously through the
vast seas in my mind.
Harsh truths like my heart
being the usual culprit for
my poor decisions.
Or like how I watch the
sun set and rise to avoid the
process of my brain settling.
Exhaustion is a drug in and
of itself.
I've grown addicted to the
routine of working my
conscience to the point where
it's too tired to think.
If you can resist the urge to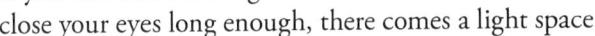
close your eyes long enough, there comes a light space.
A mental existence where your memory card is temporarily erased.
There isn't a past or future, just the now.
That is where true serenity lies, and I break out into a full-on blitz in search
of this existence every night, so it seems.
The hardest part in all of this was realizing the part I played in my own
destruction.
All the wrong turns that were made in fear of leaving my comfort zone.
Every time that I chose to ignore the things I already knew to be true.
Every time I did myself the disservice of staying in environments that no
longer suited my higher self, I added fuel to my karmic fire.
And truth be told, at this point in my life it isn't about the problems.
It's time to start producing solutions.
It's time for the healing to start.

Jill Scott "Comes to Light (Everything)"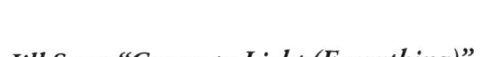

THE LIL' INSECURE HOMIE

You tuck your phone under the pillow when you creep
So, when he calls it's always fucking up my sleep
I act as if it doesn't hurt to know you fuck around and flirt
Stifled micro-aggressiveness when we speak

I don't think I'll fall in love like that again
Or trust a woman when she says "he's just a friend"
I'm emotionally exhausted from adding tallies to my losses
Like being genuine was good enough to win

The sun rises and you tell me that you love me
And I accept it because to me? I feel ugly
Because the nigga on your phone looks nothing like what I'm on
So, I laugh to deviate from how it cuts me

Remember back when I would put no one above you
And felt you melt every time that I would hug you
But now the way you say my name is cold and not the same
I feel ashamed because I hate the fact, I love you

And now I'm stuck inside a loop with all these women
Who're barely worth all the energy I give 'em
Play it cool like I like it, but you don't have to be a psychic
Just to see that I'm not *living*, just *existing*

I met a shawty who could novacane the pain
Yeah, it's cool, but it doesn't feel the same
We had linked, trynna smoke
I knew she wanted me to stroke
But when I spoke, I fucked around and said your name

Now, I'm back home pissed because I miss you
Trying not to tell the homies all our issues
So, I pack it all inside hoping one day it subsides
Cause real niggas don't need somebody to vent to

That's my defense when somebody mentions us
To deflect the fact, you have a different touch
Than anybody I've been with who barely gets my attention
Cause I look at them and find a glimpse of us

Joji "Glimpse of Us"

BE & SEE

Be the change you want to see
See the change you want to be

Harold Melvin & The Blue Notes (feat. Teddy Pendergrass) "Wake Up Everybody"

INFINITAS VIRES

I am all that I am
Because I believe I can be
The things that most people don't even see when they dream

I will climb every mountain
Embrace every fall
Welcome all adversity & victoriously stand tall

My head may be battered
My feet may get swept
But failure is one thing I'll never accept

To fail is to quit when the terror arrives
The flesh may be broken
But will never dies

J. Cole "Dollar and a Dream III"

Live in the moment

Innovation is key

Forgive all

Elevate

The Notorious B.I.G. "Sky is the Limit"

SPECIAL THANKS

MODELS

Zhanè Harrison
Thomas Daniels
The Late Lois P. Somerville
Patricia Caldwell
Lil Nola
Nefertiti
Maddie
Bubba
Juju
Zion Propst
Jody Jo

PHOTOGRAPHY
Charli Abraham
Jody Jo
Nia Terry
Zion Propst

Thank you all for being a tremendous help in bringing this idea to life.

<u>ALSO</u>
Feel free to support young black entrepreneurs:

www.ingramcontent.com/pod-product-compliance
Lightning Source LLC
Chambersburg PA
CBHW042331150426
43194CB00001B/22